ERASURES

also by Donald Revell

From the Abandoned Cities (1983)

The Gaza of Winter (1988)

New Dark Ages (1990)

Donald Revell   ERASURES

Wesleyan University Press

Published by University Press of New England ■ Hanover and London

ER-
ASU
-RES

WESLEYAN UNIVERSITY PRESS

Published by University Press of New England, Hanover, NH 03755

© 1992 by Donald Revell

Printed in the United States of America 5 4 3 2 1

CIP data appear at the end of the book

Grateful acknowledgment is made to the following magazines whose editors offered some of these poems their original publication:

Agni: On the Cape; A Type of Agnes

American Poetry Review: The Next War; Warm Days in January

Antaeus: Sirius

Arete: Muse

Gettysburg Review: Jeremiah

New American Writing: The Massacre of the Innocents; Benzene (as "The Waters of 1989")

Ohio Review: Apart from Solitude

Paris Review: Last

Poetry: An Episode of the Great Awakening in New England

River Styx: The Deposed

Southwest Review: Of Africa

Sulfur: Lesson of the Classics; Epigone; On the Cards; Heat Lightning; Anniversary of Many Cities; And Nothing But

Three Rivers Poetry Journal: The Other The Wings; The Hotel Sander

Verse: City More Than I Suspected; Explicit Vita

Willow Springs: Mayakovsky Welcomed to America, 1925

The author would like to thank the Ingram Merrill Foundation for a grant that was of great help in the completion of this book.

TO MY FRIENDS

Contents

ERASURES

Muse

You are somewhere very close to the porch.
The evening makes crazy sounds, but makes sense.
The unpackaged, greeny neighborhood settles
into true night far from the expressway
and farther from the calligrams of the downtown.
The visits to the paintings failed me.
The new music faded underground with the last trains,
with stripped hours and many lovers.

I did not imagine a stronger life,
listening for your step on the porch step,
imagining your dress a size too large
billowing the obscene print of summer.
Anything composed is an obscenity:
a painter's phlox in vertical brushstrokes,
a dressmaker's parody of stupid earth,
a radio's jazz clawed by cats.

A stronger life exists but is no one's friend.
She lives in the crook of the expressway
in a high building. She tucks her hair behind
her ears and carries a clear drink to the window.
No one ever paints her portrait. Her name
is ugly and can't be put to music.
And at her neck and ankles a long dress
blackens calligrams I read with my fingers.

The truth of those black messages is cold.
The imagination has no power over life,
and between inspirations that are lovers
and inspirations that are a kind of machinery
repainted every year but irreparable
the only thing actual at day's end
is night's uncomposed, leafy tunelessness.
I will not open the door when you arrive.

I will not call my lost loves to wish them well.
In my house in darkness behind the porch
I pound the walls and make an animal noise
as the neighborhood rises and runs en masse
onto the expressway to be destroyed
or dragged downtown to touch the calligrams
and feel nothing that is green, made, or harmonious.
It is loveless time, the neck and ankles of time.

I need more loneliness than alone is,
the deep, uninspired dark of America
where sexy lawns, the phlox, the print dresses
and hymn stanzas like tiny, circular railroads
ask for no response and no love
but a clear drink in the solitary evening
when no muse visits, when crazy animal sounds
make sense and I read the truth with my hands.

Marina Pacifica

The Lesson of the Classics

The remaining oracles were obscene,
like unfolding a towel and finding maggots there
and the next moment a detonation of green

flies. So many sexual martyrs had tied
machinery to their sallow backs, their weedy
shoulders, hoping monstrousness might revise

the brutal logarithm of excess
tenderness, of man and woman with Iphigenia
who must die, of government that must undress

the condemned in open court before they die.
The love of honor became murder.
Human, purposeful embraces at night

became machinery on a martyr's back.
If you have a family, starve them.
If your passport lies open on the desk

of a stranger, man or woman it makes no difference,
your life ended an hour ago.
There on the desk, your inverted face

in the passport photo sobs and twists
farewell as if it were already on fire.
If you have a child, you kissed

it for the last time an hour ago.
They are strapping something to its back,
the shape of an olive tree, the size of snow.

Infant spittle beads like mercury
on the temple pavement. It is an oracle,
caustic ichor of many victories.

Jeremiah

He does not shout. His voice is a perfume
sprayed into shafts of sunlight, a smell
of flowers burning too fast, too close together.

His brochures explain the rapacity of nature,
the sad inutility of the fountains
dedicated to Heine in 1900.

Heine's face is unintelligible.
The bare extremities of the Lorelei
gesture starvedly in the copper bowls,

eroded to wires and moth-metal.
Graffiti obscures obscenity with obscenities.
The sun is not a sphere.

The sun is a wall. Behind it, the police
strut gaudily as umbrella birds, and no
emergency believes in the wall.

In his hot alcove, the prophet stares unblinking,
scorching himself deeply so it may never
happen quite this way again. He says

"In the desert I prayed only for mercy,
not happiness, not vindication, willing
to settle. No price can be too high, no

cruelty excessive if the end
finds cruelty exhausted and mercy
audible as a hammer's sound in rain."

Flowers burn too fast, too close together.
Poverty is the last taste of sunlight
from 1900 where we shall meet again.

The Massacre of the Innocents

The law moves quickly in the rain
and chokes the world with memorials.
The courts accept the lowest superstition
into evidence. And we embrace quickly in the rain,
conceiving a hale infant with hands to wrinkle
the bedsheets toward it, wave by trough by wave.

We had the autumn. We had an hour
of massacre and then the wintertime.
I am beginning to believe in Fate,
in the circulation of ash inside
the bone, clattering along the pavements
like yellow shrapnel. It needs no purpose.
It needs only an engine and a name.
When you open a child, there is nothing
but a cramp of terror and a wrinkling hand.

In the unannealment of autumn, autumn shatters.
In a crow's mouth, love is a crow's mouth,
and the white percussion of faith is all the sound.
I heard it—white percussion like pianos
striking pianos, and no outrage, no transport.
Murder wrinkled its hand inside my house
that is my house no longer.

Man is weakest.
Faith chokes the world with his memorials.
Unbelief chokes the world with his nakedness.
There is no future if the past is helpless.
Let it find engines equal to these bones.

Epigone

The idol of the moment is for all time.
I love the unresilience of it,
inexpressive nudity of seawater
painted onto a car's windshield,
improvised when there was nothing to know.

You may kill the spider, but spare the web.
My son feeds at the breast like that.
His face grows smaller as his body grows.
At his level, the wind has an ant's legs,
and there is nothing to know except
the anatomies of wind changing,
acquiring flesh oh at all levels.

I depend upon the idol of the moment
as upon the unsustained, saving grace
of the night school, the yellow instructors
weeping unashamedly when none else
is moved at all. I hear the sounds
anatomized in the wind's sound,
sustained in my son's voice.

Faith is improvisation. It marks
the sky with a double helix of airplanes,
our better humanity, and fills
the interstices with a child
as the rain falls and the wind stutters
away into the shadows at an ant's pace.
Everything irreparable deserves worship,
least gesture of the wind, music.

On the Cards

Upstairs is warmer but is not the future.
Somewhere else, in a cage, the winter nations
of circus-men and half-men and refugees
are interrogated out of existence.
Upstairs, the family makes music.
But in the future's idiot containment,
questions turn to ice, and the first snow
of many deaths turns black before it falls.

Someone stirs it up inside me.
Native of the capital city,
musician's bastard, tour-guide,
she is new perfectness, and I am her creature.
Having been happy for so long
in a cage, she used up all her sex
in that cage, confessional she now
recites as we drive past the monuments.

Families make music for circuses.
Time puts an end to circuses.
In animal sentences, loveliest
time that I shall ever know, the future
increases, recites, recovers
tear-jerking horizontal landscapes
in black ice and the mercy to love
a father's vanity and not the father,
a mother's bitterness and not the mother.
Orphancy of the confessional
acquits black earth and cradle, what I was waiting for.

Heat Lightning

We are living in the beautiful district.
The wind lets no leaf touch the ground.
Next door, in bright sun, a girl on stilts
is so fabulously illuminated
she blends into the light below her legs.
We are a people without holidays.

On the old street, men would kill their wives
for a stiff wind. Their freedom was laws,
and their lives stank. No one is healthy
where discarded children return cureless
and the wind's telegraphy on flagpoles
(colonial savage other) speaks
the fates of animals, the edicts of holiday.

Concede a limb to save a limb, an eye
for an eye that looks outward only.
My heart was a sieve of law and had
no reward but my next child's slower illness
on the ward where they made Christmas in July
and every month. The stockings never came down.

On the old street, sacrifice depended
upon faith. In the beautiful district,
light stands firm beneath the children,
I live alone, undiscarded, and
sacrifice is the ordinary of each day.
Sun and wind intensify
without interruption and we blend
to one color the color of windows.

1990

The morning dares not lift its eyes. The orchid
copulating with the sightless wasp
renews its contract, its disadvantage.
We have returned to questions of the earth
so late, decades late, and death increases
the dignity of each surviving thing
unto the last disadvantage.

I do not lift my eyes. I execute
the angel of intimacy in darkness
where each word is mistaken, each brutal
affection a wasp upon my sex
sightless as the future come and gone.
Death increases. It is a real density
to be enjoyed as potency
in dismantled tenderness.

Nothing dissipates upon waking.
The dream scenarios (the hotel bars,
the success of Communism, armored flowers)
obviate the questions of the earth
never asked in custody.
None to deceive from this day forward.
None to love until another decade
blows the tiny souls aflame.
Wasp's progeny will feast on orchids.

The Deposed

As he was a boat dragged through the streets,
they turned their hoses on him.
He did not sink, not either did he reach
the isthmus of his children.
He was not the worst.

They come to power tomorrow.
By the unpated hulk, behind a rail,
beneath a bulb, their rostrums
come to power tomorrow
when sky no longer recites the sky
but rates of exchange and blue anthems.

He could still feel the impact of his borders.
They tore themselves away with sounds
of pavement scraping a keel.
He could still feel the bed-shapes of horizon,
girls shaped like extradition.
I saw the photographs fall out of his pocket.
No innocence could have been more helpless.

Seed of the heart travels poorly,
feeding on emptiness like mercury,
useless revolution of no tone.
Who rejuvenates the martyrs
rejuvenates the tyrants.
Best governs who least grieves, whose limeheart
quickens to no sound in the coming days.

Anniversary of Many Cities

Darkness undrew the air where it was naked,
poppy and dramaturge, flower and firebomb.
Too much innocence survived.
Something remnant, twilight without end
on the receding cockpits, tainted
the alcohol of orphancy. Every wall
was a shafthouse, every plume of smoke a woman
lewdly photographed by her kinsmen.

I live on credit.
I love a man, and he is meat.
I love a woman, and she is red hair,
a plume of smoke who loves me longer.
All over Europe, restorations proceed
and make a sound exactly nothing, a tone
between a whine and a detonation.

Whoever minted the coin of total war
made everything else worthless, counterfeit.
Take it to the madhouse or take it to bed,
it is still war. Getting and spending
are war. Because there is no such thing
as immortality, sufficient unto the day
are its casualties.
What does not die deserves to live.

The Next War

We have rehearsed our enemies.
Just as the lover's hand instructs its shadow
in white mystery, in dark no dark,
we have instructed our deaths in other people,
put words in their mouths, shown them how to stand.

Never in sunlight again, or ourselves in sunlight.
I was alone on the dunes, at the reading lamp
of the North Sea. Blond hair and black hair.
When it is tired, when there is no music,
history turns to its extremes, rehearses
the scene of the dagger, murder in a room
with no exit, locked from the inside.
When I am tired, my hands fall to my sides.
The dunes return to the sea, blond hair to black hair.
If my death is in another's hands,
his shadow will understand my shadow
as we lean backward out of the lamplight,
a plate of darkness, a photograph of nobody.

Racial and ethnic strife are as we taught them.
We rehearsed our enemies,
our hands buried up to the wrists in them.
The words they use will be familiar.
Their bodies will be young, transparent
inexhaustible choreography
when there is no music, locked from the inside.

Benzene

It is the right time for hallucinations.
Drowning in a sty, the sailor
feels the ocean's buoyancy.
Dying in a web, the moth
discards its wings and falls free.

I wish something would put its hands on me,
give me stronger poison and then stronger.
The beautiful flotillas do not stop.
Undying love drifts and delays.
I am capsizing.

Great joy lingers still.
Nothing can be said for suffering.
It is legible only to strangers
and at great distances. It detests
survivors. It drapes gun-carriages

with flowers, lampposts with hanging boys.
It is the right time for hallucinations,
most nakedly of inmost west.
Her death would be less tender now,
dusted over with charity,

a web of useless wings, a shallow sty.
She gave me stronger poison and then stronger.
I miss her.
In the back seat of the taxi,
dark breathlessness says "Hurry, hurry."

Erasures

City More Than I Suspected

Where Lot's wife left the train
the world's hair unraveled and fell,
not wantonly, but with the precision
of hopelessness, the dead man
who handles his cigarette and fork
like a surgeon, knowing death's weight.

Under the toque of my life
I'm begging, I'm cakewalking.
I hurdy-gurdy and my friends
become other animals
or fanatic labyrinths.
The world's hair falls too slowly,

China is unavenged,
and every child is justified
spitting from the schoolbus
when his spittle hits home.
My friend whispers the sonnet
of his first adultery into the telephone.

His baby son is an idiot,
and his wife grows large
with uncontainable loveliness
she fills with voices.
Years of idiocy
cannot stop my admiration.

Years of betrayal on the grand scale
taught China nothing.
Impossible cloud crossing the mountains,
she is perfect only
where the spittle strikes her.
Perfect only zero in Asia,

pretending to the life of a woman,
she handles her mob genitals roughly.
Where Lot's wife left the train
the salt-taste of her hair
made Heaven of hopelessness.
No one travels farther than that.

The Other The Wings

Vivid out of nowhere,
the ashen paper-smell of summer
cripples the garden.
The poor peonies
are dead of their own weight,
every wound exposed.

I went walking. In the park, the defunct observatory wore a helmet of
hot moonlight. Its basement glowed where the AA meeting, already
frantic with cigarette smoke, made exaggerated, weightless gestures
like those of astronauts on the lunar surface. Otherness is not the
prelude to meaning. The moon cures no addiction, prevents no wars.

Vivid out of nowhere,
the wind is food.
I have my key, I have my penny.
ZumZum, it is 1970,
and I am tired of my dignity.
Nothing in the world sustains it.

On the pavement, jadeweed was an island in its own shadow. Each
house along the street exposed interiors in yellow lamplight, but no
one moved inside. To see things without imagining their circum-
stances is the most difficult happiness. Red hair reaches down to the
jadeweed. Summer music begins, the nowhere passage from lighted
house to dark house.

Vivid who were frightened before,
the circumstances of physical life,
weight and wounds,
drift instead of death.
The hairy back of Arnold Schoenberg
is a moth.

I found a wad of paper and picked it up. Inside, intact and dead, a
moth, a brown sex in a white carnation. Things only fly that have
no cause, no allegiances, not even to their bodies. The effect is
catastrophic. I held a naked roof in my hand, a famished gratitude.
Before it died, the moth was not a flower. It had flown across
mountains.

Sirius

A vineleaf at the window
at night flattens
the world better
than Justinian.
A garden
is a species of policeman.

The cricket is a species of mole. When I think of loving someone new,
I feel blinded. I hear the jewels singing in the houses of my neigh-
bors, in the treetops and underground. We are all in hiding. The
deportations did not end with the war, continuing since the world
began.

The loneliness
of a man's perversion
makes him an angel.
He finds himself
touching himself with a stylus,
hearing needle music
intently out of his skin.

The enthusiast does everything he can to postpone his pleasure. He
takes the lovely soprano to a bad cafeteria in a bad museum. She sings
in spite of all, something by Brecht, high and deadpan. When she
leaves the cafeteria, her hair bounces. Nothing can be postponed any
longer. The insect vaudeville of the trains runs faster.

If on Palm Sunday
not palms but panes of glass.
A man is not an animal.
The mandibles of desire
sting through walls.
In my shirt draped on the chair
a shadow-lyre
blackens windows with its sound.

If she were small enough, in the complete darkness, she could sleep between the strings. Music untitles the Jew of summer, a species of angel. The stylus reaches all the way across the alley. Sleeping there, the perfect soprano wears every surface of her body to bed. The starlight also reaches her, no one to say otherwise.

The Hotel Sander

After the storm at sunset
the day's inconsequence
and canal, the heart of it,
is black and white.
Without a superstition
no one is a liar.

When I reached out my arm, my mother was careful, almost studious.
She would say, "It is not a piano. It is an alarm."

After the storm, only visible
an aquarium two flights up
in the son's room.
An animal whines.
An automobile brakes.
The fish ride pearls of air in the tank.

To the east of my middle years, I found a pool of water hung with
dragonflies. Stagnant under beautiful skin, the pool, more closely than
a weapon, focused my attention to the center of each breath I drew.
Erupted a fountain, green on the one hand, green on the other.

The late Dame was his widow.
It is not a negro.
It is a hairpiece.
Without a superstition,
all east surrenders to all west,
the point of travel diminishes to a climax.

When I would touch my face, my mother slapped my hand away.
The outline of leaves, missing from the pavement, bears great
responsibility for the year ahead, its stone flagon of the truth behind
the bookcase, up the hidden stair.

Each to his own veracity
rides a single pearl of air,
miserable parody of a city.
The aquarium upstairs, the storm
murders the truth also.
I was sounding an alarm.

A Type of Agnes

We must kill the street.
Dada never to know,
seized by dissent,
to speak is to disbelieve.
What they called a torch
what I spend my life with
he made at a café table
at one o'clock in the morning.

The bedroom slanted in five directions and the river took each one. It
was a toy house, took each one. At the top of the stairs, my whole life
fell into boxes. She raised a baton. She raised a river. When the waters
reached the glassworks, no pain is sharper than crystal in the lungs.

Where it was raining
he built a bicycle
underneath the cars,
silvered. I needed
desperately to return
to be lovers.
Beautiful house in shade,
who never returned
I never knew.

We must kill the street because it brings too many people forward into
light they cannot bear, into the accusations they cannot answer. If
Heaven takes an animal by the throat, it is a torch. Seized by dissent,
it invents the traffic. The selfless lesbian Geschwitz in the adagio.

Never to know
with whom I spend
my life more
in love than usual
this morning.
September little river
and little differences.
The street joins them.

The crystal furnace was rebuilt in less than a year. The river lifted a baton and the work began. No distinction is rational. I do not believe in anything, what they call a torch, silver underneath the cars. My childhood was better, dense on a blue Sunday where the water lay.

You See Corsica

Hyphen from one bondage
divides the last face loved.

At dawn, the fata morgana illusion of giant horsemen near Marseilles
abolishes the atmosphere. At such moments, any weather at all is
unbearable, a posture that cannot touch the ground. At such
moments, internal exile crackles with halogen in the bath of neolights.
Ephemeral recurring question at Montsegur: what freedom is not a
hyphen of genocide?

One could say the same
of Masada.
The last one left alive
is the traitor, the
last face to remember.
It loves a mushroom.
The vase is fire of the wise.

Enough to go around if I have stolen yours. The stick-horse in the
fallen tree is soon a rug, and what survives interrogates the poor fools,
rounds them up into camps, teaches them to sing. I am stealing from
myself. Look at Haiti, dancing above a garage. Its posture cannot
touch the ground, *faut épouser le hasard*, the beautiful tropic rising at
its center to be killed.

I do not want much longer
the fall weather
nor what will follow.
What I could not control
I could not bless.
Fata morgana
foreseen and at the same
time outlived
is a giant horseman
astride a stick-horse.

We must endure the rubbish of harmonies again. We must mutilate
the tender soul of Port au Prince again. Children, be ephemeral as you
can. Answer with halogen. As I with alcohol at Montsegur responded
to the twelve tones. When you make a sound, make it the pain bird,
mirage out of the ashes.

Explicit Vita

Throws a branch into the tree.

Only later did he learn the shrine was already incubated. He lay ill in Europe, facing a concert hall. His suitcase bulged with oranges, one for every hour until daylight and one for the train to the North Sea. On the dunes, bees hovered at ankle-level, where they remain.

Only when I close my eyes
the beautiful shirt of the composer
fills with torso
and hovers there.
October 1990.
Hallucination
melds the Germanies.
The composer dies in exile,
his mouth full of a boy,
his torso.

Amsterdam as though it were Denver. The pain worsened and the fruit filled him. If he could die, there would be life enough to cross to where the water unresists and only unfinished things, like the caffeine of oranges, touch the shrine.

I feel my way with a mop
as my mind dies
of my brain's weight
in praise of who were flayed.
The bees die at ankle-level.
The day is coming
when a beautiful shirt
will start a revolution.

And Nothing But

It is a white train
sees and makes it darker.
Oh sustain it.
I am in the wires.

What happens in the light of institutions remains profound, though
pleased too easily. The message and the man's head fingered in soap
scum fade at one distance, at the same speed. Will later drown him-
self in Paris, in the yellow of institutions, pared down to a single
holocaust fluorescent pipe.

Mister
unsaid goes to the grave,
then everything.
The use of talking
is vocable in nightmare,
perhaps only there.

An American life in five acts and an assassination. I hear the
conversation filter up to my apartment. We remember the twentieth
century as a tunnel of screens and filters. At the end, we were pure
and indistinguishable from the next man, nothing to do with yellow
cipher afloat in Paris. I just ran through my photographs to see.

The rain a much finer net
belongs to the past.
The calendar of flowers,
abyss all that you can find,
does not understand
such a reproach
such lewdness.

Her clinic is her red mane. Something filtered through her skin onto
mine. The life instead of a life glides, glides, the unwanted child
always the most histrionic. No more surprising than the leaves fall,
sky empties at the last when the air is flawless. I am in the wires.

The Ringrose

Appetite of the gunman
in the church roof
trains upon his wife
the remorse fugue the brooch
of police injury.
I envy her satiety.

Stop interrupting my death. Fugacity of the Wild Turk, but no, I've
got it backwards. I'm freezing to death and the theatre screen is huge
with lovemaking. A fugue tends every leaf of the wounds as each
becomes a winter scene: white doves balanced on a gatepost.

The lapses of a quarrel
pass for wisdom.
The aberrations of the past
trace back the way
the rain listens
in the stairwell of peonies,
yes really that far.

Rigged on a mansion (first night in the city, and then first night
again), the air recuperates. He's no murderer. Bombed into
abstraction, David Bomberg's London exceeds the orphanage of
saints, a city built on sirens.

Dragging the sound through sound,
as the spires dragged all
of Europe through a needle's eye,
the music destroys the pictures,
the gunman in the church roof
nothing interrupts.

She dies before the bullet strikes. My wristy caution, I am holding the
piano upside down, watching for the first time the ocean surface gorge
on snow. Already huge, a stray cat unpuzzles the gatepost.

Erasures

The monument is in throes.
Where such ferocity comes from
the leaf scorches,
the linen of the workers' hostel
decorates like a sunflower
in a sandpainting.

She says nothing, and it sells. The flooded stairwell undulates
limb and limb, the key of a city with no sky. The distance put
to music, my jalousie, tell me
the night was unextinguished by the lamps. The house is to let.

Out of the heart of one string
came Pierrot the Stateless.
How he rose to power,
organized the militias around
a vial of clear liquid,
scorched the linen where he lay.
Never mind. He loved always.

It was and was. I sat in a tiny airplane and the scenery defied
hallucination. Have you forgotten, composition by tones and daggers
made these beautiful valleys, these clockwork villages? Ungrateful
now, as every pharmaceutical is ungrateful to the illness, the good folk
spit into icons only the snow loves, in little mounds, in a bird's track.

Was and was.
By unexpected heat
unrounded, the balloons
rise all the same.
Our war rises all the same
though its deformities
cartoon the sky.
They distract our astonishment
from its true architecture:
in the stairwells, floodwater.

Apart from Solitude

Mayakovsky Welcomed to America, 1925

Anywhere on the continent, if you bent close,
you heard the song of birds in the radio
letting you know they were alive, they were
in climates better than yours, deeply shadowed
by brilliant sunlight, borne aloft by perfume,
taking the colors of their eyes from exhalations
of orchids in Florida, in California,
on the tennis and Barbizon islands
sheltered in the crooked Georgia coast.

And as you bent close, hearing the interviewer
pause, and then the birds in the silence,
then Mayakovsky, you could well imagine
a nation feeding itself on flowerless
nettles of futurity, fattening
its children on bits of flagstone and the dust
of crumbling facades. You could imagine
the complete absence of the tropics,
a defenceless freedom, a cello made of snow.

The idea of orchids is harder than a wall.
The failure of allegory and its kiss
to nature in the innocent forms of birds
and islands and young tennis players rising
from the death of the crowd's applause
to be tall as islands, sweetly upheld
as the sexual wide-eyed scream of parrots,
is sadder than a disgraceful polity.
Out of the jasper and jade stirring of April

the iron palm trees of human wishes
have not appeared. The future is nude. We sent
Mayakovsky to his death by drowning
in the melted cellos of betrayal.
In Paris, Napoleon erected
a plaster elephant on the site of the Bastille.
He meant to obscure the Revolution with exotica.
The statue became a city of rats. Sad future,
its monsters in ruins, its tyrants small as parrots.

Apart from Solitude

The age of consent comes early to protect
our civilian lives, to distract
us from the deeper celibacy
of governments and of nature that goes unpartnered
into winter, unafraid of death
because it has nothing to explain and no one
unto whom to be tender or merciful.

In late autumn, dark birds darken against
sunrise in the catalpa till they are a stone's weight.
The dying bee attacks the swollen spider
to no profit. Late abed against the chill
of morning, couples exchange the musty consent
of their bodies out of genuine love
and travel the long slide of the late autumn
into unhappier, deeper chills
the springtime will do nothing to warm.
Their loving consent disenfranchises them.

Which is to say they have agreed to lie apart
from solitude, man's and nature's original
crisis and tenure. I went out early
to have my winter coat on and to see my breath.
In the next street from mine, there was a child
in her bare feet staring up into the trees.
She saw the birds there, huge with stillness in the cold.
She told me they were kittens and that I
should bring them down to her. I walked away.
It was too early in the day and too early
in the unpartnered time of the girl
to explain or even tell her of the morning
of my fourth birthday when I saw what she saw
and called the kittens down. They came to me,
and I began to enjoy the feeling of love,
began that early to be dead to the world,
to have no voice in its government or nature.

An Episode of the Great Awakening in New England

As night pushes its red forerunners
onto hills serrated above Holyoke
and the Great Revival ends in protest
of delay, of quiet April slow to flower
into watchful sanity at Easter,
pushing also onto the parallax
of what is secret in the afternoon,
a few people reading, others restless
at the windows or at their smooth machines,
I name a city under my breath, feeling
its cold altars retrograde inside me.
Jerusalem. The Pilgrim ziggurat
taller than history and greeny now
like a woman above her sex and crowned
with aspirations that are all flowers.

The revivalist finds his driveway in the dusk.
I love that man. His doubts are my doubts.
Am I elected to only one life
or is there a flower without watchfulness
beautiful to everlasting
in recombinant cities warm as summer?
Can I live beyond the prices that I pay
out of my heart to the upward circuitry
of the New Jerusalem's ziggurat?
Exposed on the high places for delight,
the spring's revival sees into the valleys,
forsythia, dogwood and early apple
seeing the vanguard of a great darkness.

I find my driveway in the grainy dusk.
Behind me and above me my heart lies
exposed in Jerusalem as a bad altar
to aspiration in ugly hour.
At the lawn's edge the light from Holyoke
flecks the brown azaleas out of tangle.
A sortilege of tipsy parallax
raises temples over the silenced car
in April's messianic slow flowering.

Of Africa

The Cape was unpeopled by wind a year ago.
It pinwheeled housefronts, adults and avocations
where the sea calmed then cratered under each blow.

I've returned childless, unemployed, to show
the wrack at the water's edge a new ambition.
The Cape was unpeopled by wind a year ago,

and since that time, impoverishment has grown
a tiny Jerusalem in me, a mission
to where the sea calms then craters under each blow.

The text is noise, the pulpit a smooth stone.
Beloved wreckage, covenanters of a new nation,
the Cape was unpeopled by wind a year ago

for no good reason, and that reason now
establishes a future without victims
where the sea calms then craters under each blow.

The old life bred attachment to the old.
The new breeds hearts whose chambers are all treasons.
The Cape was unpeopled by wind a year ago
where the sea still calms then craters with each blow.

Warm Days in January

It has never been so easy to cry
openly or to acknowledge children.
Never before could I walk directly
to the center of an island city
feeling the automatism of millions
drawing one pious breath, shouldering
the sunset, holding it up in the oily
tree-line a while longer. Years ago,
I was never sad enough and nothing
but a hotel that I could tear to pieces
and reconstruct inside a shoebox
felt like home. My parents died. Their miserable
possessions washed up in other hotels,
dioramas of the febrile romantic.

I take my first lover, already
gray at her temples and more reticent
than shy, more tacit than admiring,
to the bus stop by the Jewish Museum.
We wait in the dark a long time.
She does not kiss me. She hurries
up out of the oily street onto the humming,
fluorescent podium of the last bus
where I see her a last time, not waving
to me, not lovable, erect in the freedom
we traduced years ago in our first kiss.

Never deny the power of withdrawal.
Never doubt that thought and time make things small.
Never refuse the easy exit line or prescribed
uncomprehending gesture. At childhood's end,
none can tell happiness from buoyancy.
None of it made any difference—
the patricides, the hotels ill-constructed,
the inconstant starlight of drugs and rebellion.
We are no more complicated
than our great-grandparents who dreaded

the hotel life. Like them, we seek the refuge
of warm days in January, a piety
whose compulsion is to survive according
to explicit laws no young woman adores
or young man follows with darling hunger.

On the Cape

Unchallenged purposes of summer rain
(a rotting wisteria, the late
massacres in China) obscure the ocean,
muffle the brave performances of Chile,
blacken the cottages with insects,
give few warnings. And as yet unchallenged,
these hard purposes occupy the sun
and teach the sweet mid-year new discipline.

I am hemmed in. The blunt instruments
of the moment seem too lovely to employ.
The keyboard festival is crystalline.
The performing alligators tented
with their dark clown are gorgeous children.
The elliptic, sunny dunescapes of alcohol
cup wildflowers between the rain and ocean
and are the world's frailest porcelain.

What defends the native rights of summer?
Only an alliance to strangeness. And only
the marriages of contradiction,
of clarity to the obscurest ocean,
produce the beautiful forms of action.
Schematic jewels project their outlines upward
out of plain sand into our trouble. They are
a new medievalism, new cloudless verticals.

All things climb toward the purposes
of summer rain. I defend my mother
with the percussion of keyboards, turning
the volume up high as the movie music
of Shostakovich lifts the siege of Gorky.
I defend my step-son with performing
alligators and with Florida, their hot clown.
Myself I cannot save, but alcohol

braids a flowery Chilean harness
binding me to the future where I am rescued.

For the sake of clarity, for the obscurest
ocean's sake, remember the form of action.
It is no one. It is vertical and medieval.
It is re-marriage and saves the years
from a hard discipline. Look there. Look there.
New insects. New jewels. The cottages flying open.

Last

The unsigned architecture of loneliness
is becoming taller, finding a way farther
above the horizontal flowering
of the Cold War, the peonies
and star asters of wild partisanship.
I have a shambling gait and lonely
hysteria, but no Terror. I am free
to shamble past the vacant lot of my son's
conception, to shamble past the bar where I
conceived adultery as a Terror
that would be endless, flowering
in great waves through air striated like chenille.
I walk for a long time and try to conjure
elsewhere in its early isolation.
I cannot. It is all redestinated
by the future like the loose balloons
a janitor recovers at 6 AM
from cold light fixtures. The Cold War is ending.
Buildings are taller and have no names.

1.

The romance of every ideology
torments the romance of another. How
beautifully, in the beginning, in
the gale and embrace of isolation, boys
capered over a shambles and swore oaths.
The scent of urine in the hall at home
was righteousness. The beautiful nude
obscured by dust in a paperweight
was righteousness. Neglectful townships coming
into steep flower just as boys were flowering
needed the correction of righteousness,
the horizontal slag of government
by children. Only the insane allegiances
endure. The mad counterparts are lovers
passion cannot explain nor circumstance
restrict to the dead zones of irony.
A counterpart of the end of the Cold War

is adultery. A counterpart
of loving a divided Berlin
unto death is fatherhood, the doting
maintenance of sons in vacant lots
continuing the wars of rubble
for righteousness' sake and for the sake
of nudes obscured by dust and vulgarity.

Romance torments romance. The most beautiful
moment of the twentieth century
galed and embraced the acrid smoky air
as the Red Army entered Berlin
as Hitler shriveled in the gasoline fire
as Red Army flags opened above Berlin
safeguarding the ruins of a changeless future.
Townships blackened even as they flowered.
Loose balloons cluttered the low sky and sun.
I walked for a long time and tried to conjure
the form of kindness. It was a domestic
animal confused in the tall grass.
Boys set fire to the grass. History
that opens flags opened the fire,
and Berlin, divided from Berlin,
began to love its children past all reason.

2.
My son reads sermons of pain and writes on walls.
He starves the ground
he walks on, preparing a dead city
to be worthy of its new flags, to shine
as exploded windows shine, raining down
for hours after the wrecking crews have gone.
I have a lover now who hates children.
The hatred floats inside of her, a weightless
sexual pavilion of perfect form
and perfect emptiness. I thought
by making love to her I would conceive
nothing but Terror, outrage upon outrage,
a violence that would last my whole life
and free my son. I was ignorant as a balloon.

Across the luminous expressway, I see
the shapes of charred tenements castellated,
fading into the more tender shapes of night.
It may be the last night in history. Tomorrow
pulls down the Berlin Wall, pulls down my honor,
and I return to my lover's bed to float
in a white condom, no longer my son's father.
Tomorrow describes everything in detail.
It explains nothing. It does not teach my boy
that tenements are better than the future,
better than peace, more likely to produce
brothers than are the glassy hands of mornings
without end or walls denuded of their wire.
In the dead zone of irony before dawn,
only the cats cry, like martyrs in the flame.

3.
Gates everywhere. The Brandenburg. The Great
Gate of Kiev beneath which children stride
onto an invisible crescendo
disappearing into gasoline fires,
emerging as the new shapes of righteousness
in slow vans through the Brandenburg Gate.
Oaths are secret because none suspects
that they are kept. They thrust themselves towards us
unashamedly, like the insane homeless,
and we do not see them. In our loneliness,
we see a chance for love in betrayal,
not death. In our loneliness, we see the happy
triumph of glassy hands in free elections,
not the denuding of Berlin or wanderings
of children in vans reduced by fire
to black transparencies in the morning shade.
When Joan of Arc surrendered to the flames
she cried out "Jesus, Jesus." Some years later,
a failed magician who had loved her cried out
"Joan, Joan" as the flames mocked him with a sortilege
too easy to be unreal or profitable.

I walk for a long time and try to conjure
the form of loneliness without Cold War.

It is ash upon ash, a chiaroscuro
aloft and on the ground, completely still.
Oaths are secret because none suspects
the desperation of every object, the child
in every atom of the misused world
thrust towards us, crying out whatever
sacred name it witnessed put to death
on the ascending music of a wall.
Our buildings are tall and have no names.
The parks grow glassy hands instead of flowers.

4.
Afterwards, the calm is piteous
but insubstantial as a smell of burn
that does not rise in smoke or die with the fire.
Imagine walking out of a house at sunrise
and having to invent air, invent light
from nothing but untriggered memory.
All things beloved are recalled to pain.
Air recollected from the wrists of girls
braceleted for Confirmation, crossed.
Light recollected from between the cars
of night trains in a deep river valley
where islands in the river glowed like swans.
Air recollected from a ditch in flower.
Light recollected from the sex of flowers
in bare rooms, the grainy light of blondes.
Air recollected from religion.
Light recollected from the incensed clutch
of bodies before sunrise in the oaths
of a great and ignorant lost cause.

Imagine walking out of a house at sunrise
having spent the night in bed with a stranger.
Aloft and on the ground the calm
unfurls like flags without device or slogan.
The inconsequence of the day ahead
stirs airless atmospheres in darkness
visible as daylight but without shade.
Without Cold War, without the arbitrary
demarcation of cause from cause, of light

and air from the unsexed improvisations
of memory, I cannot see to walk
or breathe to breathe. Sex becomes applause.
Sex becomes television, and the bastard
avant garde of lonely architecture
breaks ground at the unwired heart of a city
that marks the capital of nothing now.

5.

A scratchy, recorded call to prayer crosses
the alley from one new building into mine.
The consolations of history are furtive,
then fugitive, then forgotten like a bar
of music that might have been obscene or sacred
once, in another city, in the days
before today. My son is well. He works
the public ground and needs no Antigone.
My lover sits beside him at dinner,
sharing a joke, unmapping the tall future
and its unbiased children, reinventing
the sexual pavilion to accommodate
plague wards. Romance forgives romance.

The early isolation of this gorgeous
century disappears into good works.
The future is best. To put a final stop
to the grotesque unmercy of martyrdom
and to the ruinous armies of mad boys
whose government is rape, whose justice
is a wall, revoke all partisanship,
adjourn the Terror. The future is best.
It unobscures the dusty nudes. It protects
the river islands and their glowing swans.
But when I need to die, who will light the fire?
What names shall I cry out and what music
burn to a black transparency in my heart?
The unborn have been revoked. They will not be kind.

UNIVERSITY PRESS OF NEW ENGLAND publishes books under its own imprint and is the publisher for Brandeis University Press, Brown University Press, University of Connecticut, Dartmouth College, Middlebury College Press, University of New Hampshire, University of Rhode Island, Tufts University, University of Vermont, and Wesleyan University Press.

DONALD REVELL grew up in the South Bronx and graduated from the Bronx High School of Science in 1971. His degrees are from Harpur College (BA 1975), SUNY at Binghamton (MA 1977), and SUNY at Buffalo (PhD 1980).

Revell was a National Poetry Series Winner in 1982 for his first book of poems, *From the Abandoned Cities*. In 1985 he won a Pushcart Prize. His most recent collection, *New Dark Ages,* won the PEN Center USA West Award for Poetry. His other honors include a Shestack Prize from *American Poetry Review* and fellowships from the Ingram Merrill Foundation and the National Endowment for the Arts. His work has been selected for three editions of *Best American Poetry*. Revell teaches at the University of Denver and edits *Denver Quarterly.*

Library of Congress Cataloging-in-Publication Data

Revell, Donald, 1954–
  Erasures / Donald Revell.
p.   cm. — (Wesleyan poetry)
  ISBN 0–8195–2203–1 (cl). — ISBN 0–8195–1206–0 (pa)
I. Title.   II. Series.
PS3568.E793E7   1992
811'.54—dc20   92–12429

∞